READING
IN OLD PHOTOGRAPHS

To my cousin Gibb
with all my love
Lynne
xxx
17/8/98

READING
IN OLD PHOTOGRAPHS

COLLECTED BY
P. G. SOUTHERTON

Budding
BOOKS

A Budding Book

First published in 1988 by Alan Sutton Publishing Limited

This edition published in 1998 by Budding Books,
an imprint of Sutton Publishing Limited
Phoenix Mill · Thrupp · Stroud · Gloucestershire GL5 2BU

A catalogue record for this book is available from the British Library

ISBN 1-84015-054-8

Typesetting and origination by
Sutton Publishing Limited.
Printed in Great Britain by
WBC Limited, Bridgend, Mid-Glamorgan.

CONTENTS

INTRODUCTION 7

1. THE BIRTH OF PHOTOGRAPHY 9

2. STREETS AND BUILDINGS 13

3. TRADE AND INDUSTRY 49

4. SCHOOLS AND THE UNIVERSITY 75

5. TRANSPORT 97

6. READING AT WAR 109

7. PEOPLE AND EVENTS – A MISCELLANY 123

8. THE COUNTRYSIDE AROUND 147

ACKNOWLEDGEMENTS 160

INTRODUCTION

Reading is an ancient town founded in Anglo-Saxon times, or even earlier. When the Domesday survey was compiled it was but a small borough of some two hundred souls, and so it remained until the establishment here, early in the twelfth century, of a religious house destined to become one of the most important of its kind in the kingdom. The building of the great abbey, attracting as it did workers and craftsmen from a wide area, brought about a considerable increase in the number of townspeople. Before long the constant stream of visitors to the abbey on business, and to the abbey church on pilgrimage, created a demand for service industries of all kinds, stimulating trade and making Reading the largest and wealthiest town in the county. Wealth came not only from the abbey, however, but also from the wool trade which flourished in Berkshire in the thirteenth century and for some 400 years thereafter. Side by side with this, there grew up associated industries including tanning, leather and metal-working, silk and sailcloth weaving and, of course, the manufacture of woollen broadcloth.

The Civil War was to have a serious effect upon Reading. Subject to siege, bombardment and occupation by the armies of both sides, the life of the town was badly affected. Even after the ending of hostilities hard times persisted. The Corporation had been stripped of its wealth, as had most of the citizens, whilst the cloth trade, already in decline at the beginning of the war, came virtually to an end. The latter years of the seventeenth century however saw a renewal of prosperity as other industries took the place of weaving and the sale of woollen cloth. Thanks to its situation at a point where the rivers Kennet and Thames are readily fordable and where important roads cross, Reading remained an important centre of communications and commerce. Its markets served an extensive area, while the annual fairs were of national as well as local importance. With the return of economic stability the population continued steadily to increase.

Development slowed for a while in the wake of the Napoleonic Wars, but dramatic changes were not long in coming. In 1785, William Blackall Simonds established his brewery. In 1806, John Sutton opened his first seedsman's shop in the Market Place and, just a few years later, John Huntley began to make biscuits in a small shop in London Street. On such modest beginnings were laid the foundations of industries which, before the end of Victoria's reign, would make the name of Reading synonymous with 'Beer, Bulbs and Biscuits'. The opening up of the waterways, the improvement of the highways and the arrival in the 1840s of the railway changed Reading from a comfortable country market town to a centre of large-scale commerce and industry. As the town began to overflow the medieval boundaries to which it had previously been confined, the seemingly inexhaustible supply of good local clay provided the basic building material for growing residential areas. By the end of the nineteenth century the population had increased tenfold. Public health and education were now regarded as matters of importance. Water supply, drainage and the paving and lighting of the streets were organised on more modern lines. Gas and electricity supplies were provided. New industries joined the 'beer, bulbs and biscuits' in contributing to the general prosperity.

The twentieth century has seen a continuation of this growth. Fortunately Reading was less affected than many towns of comparable size by the economic depression of the 'Thirties and the ravages of the Second World War. In the post-war years the changes to the face of the town, even when measured against those of the preceding century, have been dramatic. Old and famous industries have given way to modern high technology. Small town-centre businesses have been swept aside by branches of national and multinational companies whilst office blocks have changed the skyline. As the population of the town continues to grow, so large areas of once fertile farmland are being taken up by housing developments. Places which were once villages in their own right have been swallowed up and are now viewed as neighbourhoods with little to distinguish them from any other part of the town.

It was in 1844, in a house in Baker Street, Reading, that William Fox Talbot, pioneer of the art and science of photography, set up his photographic establishment. Although his purpose was to produce plates for his photographically-illustrated books, he continued to record subjects of his choice. His Calotype prints of local buildings provide the earliest photographic views of the town. In his footsteps there has followed a succession of photographers, professional and amateur, who, in recording local scenes, have preserved for posterity a record of the changes which have taken place here in the space of the past 140 years. Thus they add a valuable dimension to historical record. In compiling this collection I have attempted to bring together, under one cover, some examples of their work.

These photographs are drawn from a variety of sources; a few from library and museum collections, many from the archives of local societies, institutions and companies. The majority, however, are from the albums of private individuals who have kindly made their treasures available to me. This compilation is not intended as a photographic history of the town presented in strict chronological order, but rather as a variety of impressions of Reading as it was in former days. Photographs of local scenes do not now have to be of any great age to depict features of the town which no longer exist and are barely remembered; hence I make no apology for some of the illustrations being of comparatively recent origin.

The Birth of Photography

WILLIAM FOX TALBOT (right) at work in his Reading Photographic Establishment in Baker Street. While he removes the lens cap of his camera to photograph his sitter, his assistant is busy copying a portrait – possibly for inclusion as a plate in William Stirling's *Annals of the Artists of Spain*. Strong sunlight was essential and photographic work was carried on out of doors in the garden behind the studio.

Fox Talbot's principal contribution to photography was the invention of light-sensitive paper and the development of the process whereby a positive print was obtained from the negative image produced by the camera.

THE ORACLE, MINSTER STREET, 1846. Established in 1628 by the will of John Kendrick, The Oracle comprised a range of workshops to provide employment for clothiers who had fallen upon hard times as the cloth trade declined. In addition to the weaving of broadcloth, sailcloth was woven here, as were sacking and silk ribbon. The buildings fell into decay and were demolished in 1850; today only the name remains. The white building to the right, an inn, survives as Cartoon's Wine Bar. Between the gateway and the inn was a small lock-up for petty offenders.

A CORNER OF ELDON SQUARE, 1846. Built of Bath stone, these houses have changed little over the past 140 years. This photograph and that of The Oracle (above) were printed from waxed paper negatives. The care and thought which went into their production is clearly evident.

PROFESSIONAL PHOTOGRAPHY. As other inventors built upon Fox Talbot's discoveries the photographic process became faster and more reliable. Within a few years several professional photographers had established themselves in the town. Despite the absence of artificial light and the unsophisticated nature of their equipment the results were very creditable.

Above are specimens of the popular 'carte-de-visite' photographs by three of Reading's photographic pioneers: Francis Dann of Broad Street, Edward Butler of St Mary's Butts and Thomas Wood of Castle Street.

LANDMARKS NEW AND OLD. The east wing of Reading Gaol framed by the doorway of the chapter house of Reading Abbey – a photograph by Sidney Victor White, a nineteenth-century photographer whose legacy is a record of the town as it once was.

Streets and Buildings

READING TOWN CENTRE, an aerial photograph of the early 1920s. Broad Street, King Street and Kings Road run diagonally from left to right across the picture. To the right of the Market Place the extent of Sutton's premises is clearly visible.

BROAD STREET in the latter years of Victoria's reign. Prominent on the corner of Minster Street is Walsingham House, an Elizabethan building demolished in 1905. At this time it was the Speedwell Motor Car Company's showroom. Queen Victoria Street has yet to be cut. In the centre of the road stands the statue of George Palmer erected in 1890 in honour of one of the town's greatest benefactors.

TWO VIEWS OF BROAD STREET, 1904. The architectural style is mainly exhuberant Victorian with red terracotta decoration much in evidence. Among the few older buildings still surviving is the Post Office Tavern (now Silvers, tailors) on the corner of Chain Street. The shops were mostly small and predominantly family-owned. The electric trams, which had only the year before replaced the horse-drawn cars, were immensely popular.

BRANCHES OF THE LARGER CHAIN STORES were making an appearance by the early 1930s: Woolworth and H. Samuels to the left; Boots the Chemists to the right. Centre left is The Vaudeville Theatre, one of the town's more popular cinemas and a principal attraction since the '20s.

THE LATE THIRTIES and Broad Street has taken on a familiar appearance. Although the tram-lines are still in place, the trolleybus is now the modern way to travel. To the right is the imposing entrance to the covered market.

ST MARY'S CHURCH AND ST MARY'S BUTTS, 1913. Reading's oldest church, St Mary's has timbers from Reading Abbey in its roof. The cottages with which it was once surrounded were removed in 1886 to give an unobstructed view of the church.

ST MARY'S BUTTS, 1886. In former times the men of the parish gathered at the archery butts here on Sundays to practice shooting for the defence of the realm. The gabled building to the left is the Swan Inn which stood at the corner of Hosier Street. Within months of this photograph being taken, these picturesque but tumbledown buildings were demolished.

THE YIELD HALL. On the banks of the Kennet at the end of Yield Hall Lane stood the sixteenth-century Guildhall, the meeting place of the medieval Guild Merchant of Reading. Being close to where the washerwomen worked, the noise of the 'bateldores' with which they beat the linen proved beyond the endurance of the Mayor and Corporation, who were in consequence allowed to transfer their hall to the former church of the Grey Friars. In latter days, prior to its demolition in the 1930s, the building formed part of John Wilder's ironworks.

THE OLD TOWN HALL. This eighteenth-century building was incorporated by Waterhouse into his New Town Hall and thus was retained for civic and public functions. To the left is the former St Laurence's Vicarage; to the right the house of Mr Blandy, solicitor, which served as lodgings for the judges presiding at the Berkshire Assizes.

THE NEW TOWN HALL at the turn of the century. Designed by Alfred Waterhouse in 1872 to replace a building which was by that time quite inadequate for its purpose, the New Town Hall was a symbol of civic pride.

THE ART GALLERY, PUBLIC LIBRARY AND ASSEMBLY HALL in pristine condition around 1895. The large assembly hall was built 1879–1882 as an extension of the Town Hall. The library and art gallery followed in 1894 filling a hitherto empty corner site.

FRIAR STREET, 1912. The Queen's Hotel (left) was replaced by the General Post Office in 1922. The Wheatsheaf Hotel and the premises at the corner of Blagrave Street were redeveloped in 1929. Blandy's ornate office adjacent to the Town Hall was to be destroyed in the air raid of February 1943.

TWENTY YEARS ON. Friar Street from the corner of Station Road. Dating from the early eighteenth century, the ivy-clad house at No. 16 recalls times when this street was favoured by lawyers and the professional classes. This building together with Barclay's Bank on the corner was demolished in 1953.

OXFORD STREET (later Oxford Road) in 1882, looking westwards from Broad Street. To the left, on the corner of St Mary's Butts, is the White Hart; to the right, at the corner of West Street, stands the Fox Inn. The tram-lines set in cobblestones are for the horse-drawn cars of the Reading Tramway Company.

WEST STREET CORNER c. 1920. The Maypole Dairy occupies the site of the Fox Inn. On the opposite corner is the Vine Hotel.

THE WHITE HART, built in 1932 to replace the original inn which was demolished when the Butts was widened. This was in turn pulled down in 1972 to make way for the Butts Shopping Centre (now the Broad Street Mall).

ST MARY'S BUTTS, READING.

THE APPROACH TO WEST STREET CORNER FROM ST MARY'S BUTTS. The constriction of the roadway at this point is clearly visible. The small building to the right, which once housed an amusement arcade and rifle range, remains almost unchanged to the present day.

GUN STREET has changed little over the past 80 years. Next to the Crossed Keys is Poynder's printing works.

LONDON STREET, 1910. A busy thoroughfare lined with small shops and a number of former town houses.

THE NORTH SIDE OF BROAD STREET, 1901. This whole range of buildings was demolished later that year to create a new road linking the main shopping area with the railway stations (there were two). At No. 34 are the original premises of Milward & Sons, boot and shoemakers. This firm moved to the opposite side of the street where it remains to the present day; one of the very few family businesses left in the town centre.

QUEEN VICTORIA STREET, 1903. This newly-developed street with its twin rows of shops, striking in dark red brick relieved with yellow, provided not only easier access to the railway, but added a new dimension to the shopping centre.

CASTLE STREET in the early years of the present century was a busy shopping street serving a densely populated area of the town. St Mary's Chapel sports a curious bell tower known affectionately as 'the pepper box'. This became unsafe and was removed in the 1950s.

Jackson's Corner, Reading.

JACKSONS CORNER, 1914, and a recruiting drive for the Territorial Army is in progress. Jacksons and the adjacent buildings have changed little in the ensuing years. Beyond the corner of the Abbey Square can be seen the York House public house and Cocks Reading Sauce factory.

MARKET PLACE.   READING.

THE MARKET PLACE, 1903. Open-air markets were held here from medieval times until 1973. The ancient timber-framed buildings near the corner of Friar Street survive, but many old buildings including Sutton's Royal Seed Establishment (right) were lost in the hurricane of development which swept the town in the '60s and '70s.

READING ABBEY. Built in the twelfth century, desecrated in the sixteenth. Children now play where the monks' dormitory once stood. In the background are the walls of the Chapter House, on many occasions the meeting place of Parliaments.

THE INNER GATEWAY is the only remnant of the great Benedictine abbey remaining intact. Through long neglect it suffered a partial collapse in 1860, but was restored in 1861–2 by Sir Gilbert Scott, architect. To the left are the long-vanished town houses of Abbot's Walk; to the right, the Assize Courts.

THE BRONZE CANNON, a relic of the Crimean War, which surmounted Forbury Hill until requisitioned for its metal during World War II.

NO. 22, THE FORBURY. A fine seventeenth-century town house. Demolished in 1962, this building in common with many old houses in the area had been acquired by the County Council for use as offices.

ST JAMES RC CHURCH. By Pugin in uncharacteristic Norman style. The church is built mainly of flint and stone from Reading Abbey, within the boundaries of which it stands. To the right is the presbytery and St James School.

THE FORBURY GARDENS. Part of the abbey lands, this area was largely a rubbish tip until acquired by the Reading Board of Health in 1862 and laid out as public gardens. In the background are the houses of Abbots Walk, all but two of which have been demolished to make way for office development.

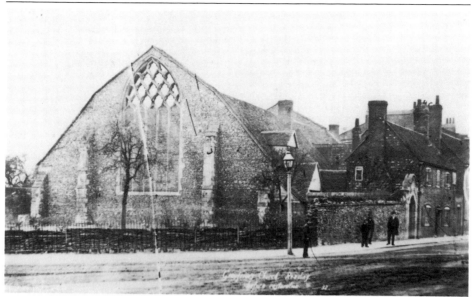

RUINOUS AND DERELICT. Greyfriars c. 1860. Built in 1288, the former church of the Franciscan or Grey Friars was given, at the time of the Dissolution of the religious houses, to the Corporation for use as a Guild Hall. From early in the seventeenth century until the mid-nineteenth it served as the local house of correction and bridewell. The building opening on to Friar Street was the keeper's house.

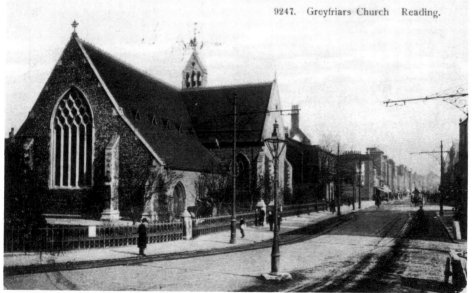

9247. Greyfriars Church Reading.

GREYFRIARS RESTORED. Having dreamed for many years of restoring the ruin as a place of public worship, the Revd William Phelps was eventually able to realise his ambition. Extensively rebuilt, the restored church was re-consecrated in 1863.

CHRISTCHURCH, built in 1860 and enlarged in 1874. The spire can be clearly seen from great distances across the Kennet valley.

KENDRICK ROAD c. 1900. The spire of Christchurch closes the rising vista of this tree-lined avenue of late nineteenth-century upper-class residences.

THE DISPENSARY. Founded in 1802, the Dispensary provided medical treatment for people of low income who would otherwise have been denied help. The Dispensary building in Chain Street, which dates from 1848, was demolished in 1976 when Heelas' store was rebuilt.

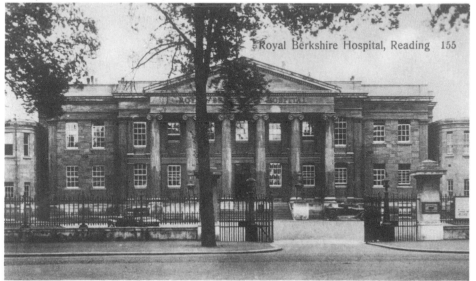

THE ROYAL BERKSHIRE HOSPITAL in the mid '20s. Built in 1839 of Bath stone brought to Reading by the Kennet & Avon Canal, the central section was designed by the architect Henry Briant. The wings were added in 1881–2.

33

A WARD IN THE 1880s. The plants, pictures and other ornaments are very much at variance with the popular image of a hospital ward in the Victorian era.

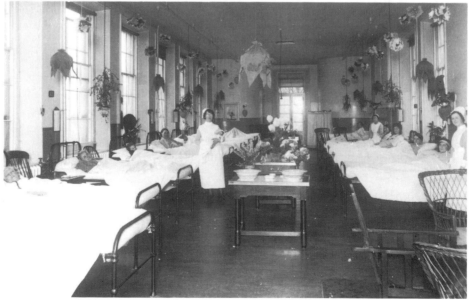

THE WARDS are laid out in a more formal manner by 1926. The austerity is however relieved here by the Christmas decorations.

484. Southern Hill, Reading.

SOUTHERN HILL. A group of early nineteenth-century residences off Redlands Road. Sadly these listed buildings fell into disrepair and were demolished in 1975.

KINGS ROAD in the 1920s, still lined by the houses of professionals and businessmen. To the left is the Italianate tower of Wycliffe Church. In the distance are the gates of the cemetery, opened as a private venture in 1843 when the town's churchyards were too full for further burials.

CEMETERY JUNCTION where Kings Road and London Road converge. To the left is the Marquis of Granby (now Hatton's) on the site of an earlier inn reputed to have been called the Gallows Tavern. The Jack o' Both Sides has yet to be built. To the right, with its imposing clock tower, is the Co-operative Society's departmental store dating from 1900.

ALBERT ROAD, NEW TOWN. Tucked away between the Kennet and Kings Road, New Town was developed to provide housing for the workers at Huntley & Palmer's factory. Much of the area was cleared in 1975 for modern housing development. In the background is New Town School, built in 1875, which, having survived the demolition, continues to serve the neighbourhood.

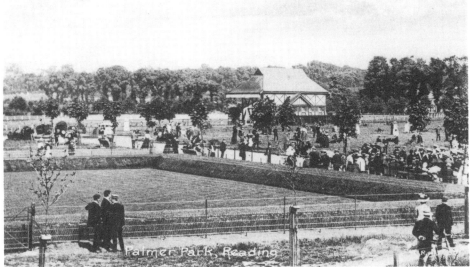

PALMER PARK. 49 acres of land in east Reading were given in 1890 by George Palmer to provide an open space and sports facilities in a heavily-populated area of the town. In acknowledgement of his many services to the town, he was made the first Honorary Freeman of the Borough.

Prospect Park,
Reading.

PROSPECT PARK was acquired by the Corporation in 1901 to provide a public open space to the west of Reading. In the summer of 1917 the paddling pool proved popular with the children.

Palmer Park, Reading.

MJR.B. 3032

THE CHILDREN were well catered for, too, at Palmer Park with a variety of swings, slides and other amusements.

16068   ST. GILES CHURCH.   READING.

ST GILES CHURCH AND SOUTHAMPTON STREET, 1905. Except for a parked governess cart and a solitary tram toiling up the hill to Whitley Street, there is not a vehicle to be seen on this main highway into Reading.

Reading. Coley Avenue.

COLEY AVENUE in the early years of the present century. Once the entrance to the drive leading to Coley House, the arched pillars (demolished in 1967) are surmounted by wyverns, the crest of the Monck family.

BATH ROAD, the main road from Reading to the west. Good-quality detached houses began to spread along this road after the removal, in 1864, of the turnpike gate situated near the junction with Tilehurst Road.

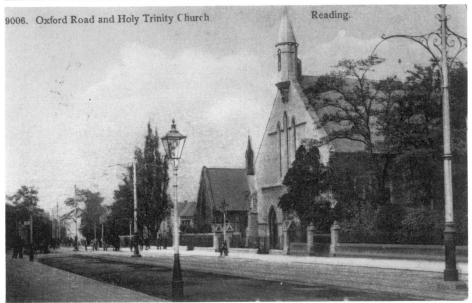

9006. Oxford Road and Holy Trinity Church   Reading.

HOLY TRINITY CHURCH, OXFORD ROAD, 1905. Built in 1826, this church has catacombs which, until intramural burial was forbidden later in the century, were used as family vaults.

132 Oxford Road, Reading

OXFORD ROAD, 1906, looking westwards from the junction with Western Elms Avenue. A parade of shops already serves this rapidly-growing residential area. The electric trams run as far as the Pond House.

WESTERN ELMS AVENUE. Until the population explosion of the 1890s, this quiet residential avenue marked the extremity of Reading's urban development.

ELM PARK HALL. Conspicuous in red brick, this Methodist mission hall, which even today towers above the surrounding buildings, is formally opened on 1 February 1905, by the Revd Sylvester Whitehead in the presence of the Mayoress of Reading, Mrs A.H. Bull.

OXFORD ROAD, C. 1907. The low arch of the railway bridge was a hazard to tram passengers on the open upper deck. The trams could not however be enclosed because of the height restrictions imposed by the bridge.

The Barracks, Oxford Road, Reading

BROCK BARRACKS, 1907. Built in 1877, the barracks was the home of the Royal Berkshire Regiment, until amalgamation in 1959 with the Wiltshire Regiment, to form the Duke of Edinburgh's Royal Regiment.

A LANDMARK IN THE MAKING. The water tower in Park Lane, Tilehurst, was built in 1931 to improve the domestic water supply to the town. This reinforced concrete structure is 115 feet in height and has a capacity of 200,000 gallons. Water from adjoining reservoirs is pumped to the tank by two electric pumps in the base of the tower.

THE MEDIEVAL CAVERSHAM BRIDGE. Breached in the Civil War, the demolished arches on the Reading side were replaced by a drawbridge and later by the iron structure seen in this photograph. By the 1860s the bridge had become quite unsafe and was inadequate even for the traffic of the day. The white building on the island in mid-stream is the ferryman's cottage.

THE BRIDGE REBUILT. In 1869 the old bridge was replaced by a functional iron bridge. In the course of its construction the three-storey ferryman's cottage was moved bodily several feet to the right. It is said that this was undertaken without so much as a pane of glass being cracked.

THE APPROACH TO THE IRON BRIDGE. To the left is the Caversham Bridge Hotel, a popular mooring for boating weekenders. The drinking fountain now stands near the riverside promenade to the rear of the hotel. The tram-lines mark the terminus of the Caversham route.

THE VIEW DOWNSTREAM FROM THE BRIDGE. Between the wars the lido on the Caversham bank was popular with bathers during the summer months. Boating, too, was much enjoyed, and punts, skiffs and other light craft could be hired by the hour or by the day from Cawston's boat-house on Piper's Island.

THE NEW CAVERSHAM BRIDGE. Built at a cost of £71,000, the new bridge was formally opened by HRH the Prince of Wales in June 1926. The structure is of ferro-concrete, the only natural stone being the parapet walls of Aberdeen granite.

READING BRIDGE. When opened in October 1923, the single ferro-concrete span of 600 feet was the largest of its kind in the United Kingdom. Whilst pedestrians using the towpath were able to pass under the bridge by way of a short tunnel, provision had to be made for the horses which were still employed on occasion to tow barges. A walkway supported on piles had to be built for this purpose.

EEL BUCKS AT CAVERSHAM. Specially-woven baskets were lowered into the water at certain times of the year to trap migrating eels. The landlord of The Griffin had the right to these bucks which were situated on an island near Caversham Bridge.

CAVERSHAM LOCK in the 1930s. Built in 1875 to replace an earlier pound lock. In 1966 the manually-operated gates and sluices were converted to hydraulic power and the keeper's house rebuilt.

Trade and Industry

HUNTLEY & PALMER'S FACTORY, 1864. Sacks of flour arrive by road. Before the end of the century the small bakery and confectionery business, established in 1841 by Thomas Huntley and George Palmer, had grown to be the largest manufacturer of biscuits in the world and one of Britain's leading industrial companies.

THE FACTORY AND OFFICES, 1900. By this time there were no less than five manufacturing units between Kings Road and the Great Western Railway line. The company was by far the greatest employer of labour in the town.

BISCUIT CUTTING, 1900. Dough rolled into sheets was passed through machines which stamped out the biscuits. Despite mechanisation, biscuit-making was a labour-intensive process. At this time the factory employed 5,400 workers whose average weekly wage was 18s 8d (94p).

H & P GIRLS LEAVING WORK. Hardly a man in sight, it being a strict rule that male and female workers should leave the factory at different times.

HUNTLEY & PALMER'S — an unfamiliar view of the bakery from the Kennet, c. 1950. Biscuit production ceased in 1976 and the whole factory, with the exception of the office block, has been cleared for redevelopment as an industrial park.

WHERE THERE ARE BISCUITS ONE MUST HAVE TINS. The ironmonger's shop in London Street from which Huntley, Boorne & Stevens Ltd., one of the largest manufacturers of biscuit tins and other metal containers, was to grow.

METAL BOX MAKING. The ironmongery business soon took second place to the manufacture of tin boxes for Huntley & Palmer's products. Huntley, Boorne & Stevens was soon to occupy a 4½ acre site between London Street and Southampton Street.

MR. GEORGE WILLIAM PALMER, M.P.

SONS OF FAMOUS FATHERS. George William Palmer (left) and Martin John Sutton (right) carried on their respective family businesses and the tradition of service to the community. Both were made Freemen of the Borough in 1902.

SUTTON'S ROYAL SEED ESTABLISHMENT. Martin Hope Sutton could not have chosen a better site than Reading's Market Place when, in 1837, he opened his seedsman's shop. Gaining a reputation for quality and reliability, the venture soon flourished and by the end of the century the premises to the rear of the shop covered an area of almost six acres.

AN ADVERTISING CARD, c. 1900, making the point that Sutton's customers enjoyed better harvests than their neighbours.

AN AIRCRAFT, developed by Miles and built at their Woodley Aerodrome factory, proved a valuable contribution to the Royal Air Force during the Second World War. Many hundreds of pilots learned the rudiments of flying in the Miles Magister Trainer.

SIMONDS BREWERY viewed from the Kennet c. 1925. William Simonds established his brewery on this site in 1795 when malting was Reading's industrial speciality. Simonds remained a family company until the merger in 1960 with the London brewers, Courage and Barclay Perkins.

THE COOPERS' SHOP. Until the advent of the alloy cask, a stock of well-made wooden barrels was essential. Simonds, as all large breweries, employed a staff of skilled coopers whose methods, materials and customs had changed little from medieval times.

BROADBEAR BROS. PROVIDENCE TIN WORKS, Audley Street, 1908. Established in the late nineteenth century, this family business produced a wide range of pots, pans and other domestic metalwork.

BROADBEAR BROS. The machine shop c. 1926.

S. & E. COLLIER LTD., brick and tile works, Grovelands. From the plentiful supply of local clay this works produced a sandy red brick known as 'Collier's Reading Red'. There were some sixteen kilns on the site producing bricks, tiles and terracotta items.

To the right is the building housing the large Hoffman kiln capable of firing a load of 20,000 bricks. To the left, the tile factory.

STACKING GREEN BRICKS. Brickmaking was a labour-intensive industry, many of the processes being carried out by hand or with the most basic of machinery. This labourer is stacking unfired bricks which he has brought from the drying shed by barrow, c. 1930.

A LIFT BOY IN THE BRICK SHEDS. C. 1930. Electric lifts to convey materials to and from the upper floors represented a concession to modernisation.

THE AERIAL ROPEWAY. As the clay in the immediate vicinity of the brickworks became exhausted, supplies had to be brought from further afield. The chain of buckets passing overhead to the Grovelands works from the claypits in Westwood Lane was for many years a familiar landmark.

THE TERMINUS, WESTWOOD LANE, from where the loaded buckets were dispatched to the brickworks at Grovelands Road, the chimneys of which are visible in the distance.

HEELAS' ORIGINAL SHOP, Minster Street, 1854. In that year John Heelas bought a small drapery shop in what was then an important shopping thoroughfare. Joined by his sons, John and Daniel, the business flourished and, within a few years, departments for carpets, furniture and funerals were added.

HEELAS, BROAD STREET, 1929. As the business grew, Heelas swallowed up other shops, cottages, a church, a school, almshouses and at least two pubs. With the purchase of the Black Boy, Heelas broke through into Broad Street to become the town's largest department store.

HEELAS' FURNITURE DEPARTMENT, 1887. Quantity as well as quality is the keynote. One wonders how the chairs suspended from the ceiling were recovered.

A DISPLAY OF MONUMENTAL MASONRY in Heelas' funeral department, 1926.

MARKS & SPENCER, 12 Broad Street. Marks & Spencer was the first of the national chain stores to open a branch in Reading. The first shop, lock-up premises in West Street, was opened in 1904. A second store opened in Broad Street in 1912, where adjacent properties were acquired as they became available and further departments added. The West Street shop became redundant and was closed in 1936. The Broad Street store on the other hand has continued to expand and has broken through into Friar Street, Cross Street and Market Way.

THE WEST STREET BRANCH, 1904. Following the pattern of the original 'Penny Bazaar', the customer was invited to walk in to inspect the wares on display.

THE STAFF OF THE BROAD STREET BRANCH, 1912. This second shop was similar to that in West Street. Some idea of the variety of goods stocked at this time may be gathered from the items on display outside.

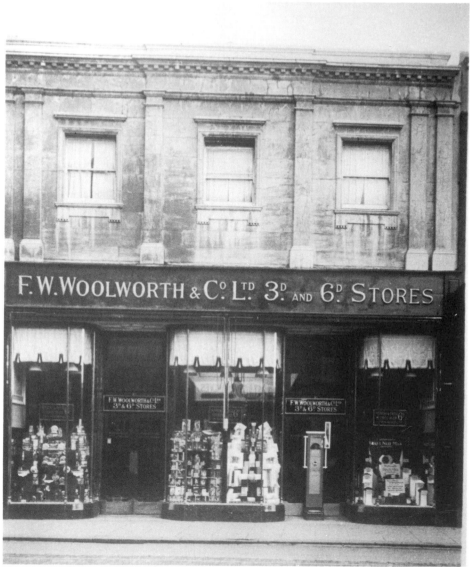

'WOOLLIES'. Woolworth's store, where nothing exceeded 6*d*. in price, opened in Broad Street in 1923. Modernised in 1932, the shop suffered a disastrous fire shortly after it had reopened. Woolworth moved to larger premises on the present site in 1939.

THE READING INDUSTRIAL CO-OPERATIVE SOCIETY. Founded in 1860, the Co-op, whilst having shops in and around Reading, had no focal point until 1928 when the Society built as its 'flagship' a new emporium and administrative headquarters at the corner of Cheapside and Friar Street. The modern lines of this new building were in complete contrast to those of the adjacent McIlroy's. On the first floor was a cafe and a large assembly hall. Another feature of the building was an arcade which ran from Cheapside to West Street.

FRANK E. MORING, wholesale confectioner, Caversham Road. From 1895 until 1958 this firm was well-known for its 'Reading Sweets'. In addition to confectionery, there were wholesale departments for haberdashery, stationery, groceries and chemists' sundries.

BOTLEY & LEWIS, watchmakers and jewellers, King Street. At the time of this photograph (1909), the business had been in existence for a century. The style of window display is typical of the period, it being felt that if the goods were not on show, the customer would not buy.

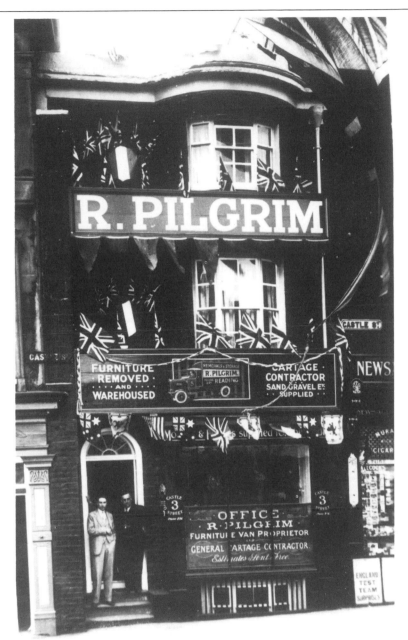

MESSRS R. PILGRIM, haulage contractors, Castle Street, decorated for the Silver Jubilee of King George V and Queen Mary in 1935.

EDWIN HEDGCOCK, drapers, Broad Street, in 1905. The premises of this family business were demolished in 1938 to make way for Woolworth's new store.

ODDMENTS, Oxford Road. The obscured windows of this old second-hand shop make the passer-by wonder what curiosities are concealed within.

McILROY'S DEPARTMENTAL STORE, Oxford Road. Because of the large amount of glass used in its construction, this grandiose early Edwardian building was dubbed 'Reading's Crystal Palace'.

GEORGE HOOKHAM'S furniture store, Chain Street, 1893. This shopkeeper, too, believed in displaying as much of his stock as possible; even going so far as to show perambulators in the upstairs windows. It is difficult today to imagine Chain Street lined on both sides with busy shops.

TUNBRIDGE, JONES & CO., mineral water factory, Castle Street, in the early 1920s. At this time shops and manufacturing premises flourished side by side in a street which is today lined on the one side by offices and on the other by the police HQ and the courts.

BUTLER'S, Chatham Street, 1902. This old-established firm of wine and spirit merchants was for many years well known for its trade name, 'Old Abbey'. Modernised, the premises are now The Butler public house.

BEFORE ....

.... AND AFTER

WELDALE MOTORS, Chatham Street, before and after modernisation in 1938. Petrol was on sale at 1s. 5d. (8p) per gallon, whilst covered parking cost 6d. (2½p) per day. These premises, which stood on the corner of Chatham Street and Caversham Road, were demolished when the Inner Distribution Road was laid out.

Schools and the University

READING'S LAST SCHOOL BOARD. The elected school boards were abolished in 1903 in favour of the new local education authorities. Among the members of the last board were Mr Arthur Newbury (back row, second from right), Mr E.P. Collier (seated at table) and Miss Edith Sutton (front row, second from left) who, in 1907, was the first woman to be elected to the Borough Council.

GIRLS OF GROVELANDS SCHOOL, 1934. Needlework class for the dressmakers of tomorrow.

NEW TOWN SCHOOL, 1934. Boys busy making model aeroplanes from plasticine, having paid a visit to an air display at Woodley Aerodrome.

CHILDREN OF SHINFIELD SCHOOL carry on the old custom of dancing around the maypole on the village green, 1934.

READING SCHOOL. In this view of East House and the terrace dating from 1890, ivy has already softened the lines of the brickwork of the new buildings opened in 1871. Dating from 1486 or earlier, Reading School is the oldest surviving institution in the town.

THE MANUAL SKILLS WORKSHOP, 1916. This well-equipped workshop, in a school which at the time offered a classically-oriented education, shows the curriculum to have been by no means narrow.

'BIG SCHOOL', 1916. Plaques around the walls of the hall record the names of famous Old Boys of the school, including Archbishop William Laud, Daniel Blagrave and Sir Thomas Noon Talfourd.

THE CHAPEL in 1916, the spiritual heart of the school which owes its origins to Reading Abbey.

READING SCHOOL FOOTBALL TEAM, 1887. Jerseys and socks are in blue and white. Breeches or shorts reach well below the knee. The day of the studded boot has not yet arrived.

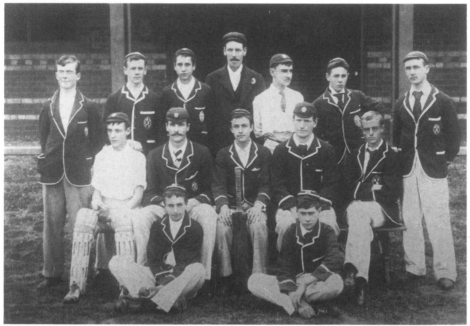

CRICKETERS, 1897. The cricket field, some eight acres in extent, was at this time regarded as one of the best in the county.

READING BLUE COAT SCHOOL, Bath Road. Established in 1660, the school moved from London Road to Brunswick House, Bath Road, early in the nineteenth century. In the niches at first floor level are figures, one of a boy in the traditional blue coat, the other in the green garb of Thomas Malthus' School which later amalgamated with the Blue Coat School. These prized effigies are now preserved at Holm Park, Sonning, to which the school transferred in 1947.

BOYS OF THE BLUE COAT SCHOOL, 1890, in traditional costume. The gown and breeches are still worn on certain formal and ceremonial occasions by boarders at the school. The headmaster at this time was Mr James Mumford, noted for his strict discipline.

PUPILS AND STAFF, KENDRICK GIRLS' SCHOOL, 1921. Schools for boys and girls were established in 1875 from the remaining portion of John Kendrick's charity. The boys' school was in Queens Road; the girls were accommodated in Watlington House.

WINNING HOCKEY TEAM, 1925.

LAYING THE FOUNDATION STONE of the new Kendrick School. By the 1920s the school had outgrown Watlington House and a new school was built in the grounds of Sidmouth House. The foundation stone was laid by Dr J. Watts, Vice-Chancellor of the University of Oxford on 17 February 1926. To the right of the mace bearer is the headmistress, Miss Prebble.

PUPILS IN FORMAL ATTIRE make their way from Watlington House to attend the ceremony.

QUEEN ANNE'S SCHOOL, CAVERSHAM, established in 1894 with 33 girls, derives its origins from the Grey Coat Hospital Charity School founded in Westminster in the seventeenth century. The school premises formerly housed a boys' school, Amersham Hall. The chapel (right) was added in 1909.

STAFF AND PUPILS, summer term, 1894.

QUEEN ANNE'S SCHOOL. The prefects, 1900.

HEMDEAN HOUSE, CAVERSHAM. Established in 1862 for young ladies, Hemdean House was set in extensive grounds. One of the highlights of the school year was haymaking in the late summer followed by the annual Hay Tea.

ST JOSEPH'S CONVENT SCHOOL, founded in 1901 by Revd Mother Mary of Calvary, for Catholic girls up to the age of 17 from good middle-class backgrounds. At this time the school was in Bath Road.

St-JOSEPH'S CONVENT

BROAD OAK, the large residence in Upper Redlands Road to which the school moved in 1909 and which forms the nucleus of the present day St Joseph's Convent School.

CAVERSHAM PARK. Built in 1850, the mansion replaced an earlier house which was destroyed by fire. The premises were acquired in 1922 by the Oratory School which moved here from Edgbaston. Upon the school moving in the early years of the Second World War to its present home at Woodcote, the mansion was taken over by the BBC for use by the Monitoring Service.

THE ORATORY SCHOOL. The grand scale of the principal rooms of the mansion proved eminently suitable for the school which was founded in 1859 by Cardinal Newman 'for Catholics of the Upper Class.'

THE UNIVERSITY EXTENSION COLLEGE from which the University of Reading was to grow. Founded in 1892, the college was originally housed in part of the former hospitium of the abbey and in the former St Laurence's vicarage.

DAIRYING AND CHEESE-MAKING LABORATORY. A Department of Agriculture was established within the college in 1893 just as British farming was recovering from the depression of previous years. The Faculty of Agriculture and Horticulture was to become the largest and most complex centre of teaching and research in these subjects in the United Kingdom.

ART AT THE UNIVERSITY COLLEGE. (Above) A ladies' modelling class, c. 1900. (Below) A mixed class of students. Academic dress was obligatory at all lectures and most classes.

THE MAIN ENTRANCE, London Road, 1906. The buildings in Valpy Street proved inadequate for the growing College. A timely and generous gift of property by the Palmer family, however, provided a larger site in London Road.

THE OLD RED BUILDING (centre), the first of the buildings already on the London Road site to be used by the college. To the left is the Department of Music; to the right, Portland Place, acquired later for college use.

THE FIRST STEP TOWARDS THE ESTABLISHMENT OF AN INTEGRATED COMMUNITY. The ceremonial laying by Viscount Goschen, Chancellor of the University of Oxford, of the foundation stone of the Great Hall, 1905.

THE GREAT HALL, 1910. As a setting for functions, formal and informal, the hall was the very heart of the college.

THE LIBRARY, 1906. Situated on the upper floor of The Acacias, the former home of George Palmer, the college now had the benefit of a well-stocked library.

WANTAGE HALL. Endowed by Lady Wantage, this hall of residence, providing study-bedrooms for 75 students, was opened in October 1908. This view of the dining hall from the arch of the turretted gatehouse is evocative of an Oxford quadrangle.

TWO VIEWS OF ST ANDREWS HOSTEL. The first hostel for women students was established in 1900 by Miss Mary Bolam as a private venture. In 1911, with the status of College Hall, St Andrews moved into Alfred Palmer's former house in Redlands Road. The original building in London Road was later used by the Borough Council as a children's home and adult training centre until its demolition in 1976.

THE BELL TOWER UNDER CONSTRUCTION. Erected as a permanent and visible memorial to those members of University College who gave their lives in the Great War, the tower is 61 feet in height and 14 feet square at the base. The greater part of the building work was undertaken by the local firm of Collier & Catley.

DEDICATED IN JUNE 1924, the tower houses a bell weighing over 2½ tons which serves both to strike the hour and to summon the congregation of the University. It was a tradition that on 11 November the bell sounded 144 times to commemorate the fallen whose names are inscribed on bronze plaques in the base of the tower.

DR W.M. CHILDS, principal of University College, chaired by joyful students in 1926 after his announcement that the charter affording the college full university status had at last been granted.

WHITEKNIGHTS PARK. The entrance, 1910. The problems of overcrowding suffered by the University in post-war years were solved by the purchase in 1958 of Whiteknights Park, the final remnant of the medieval manor of Earley.

WHITEKNIGHTS HOUSE, one of the six large houses built when Whiteknights Park was first sub-divided and let. When acquired by the University, Whiteknights House was altered to accommodate the then infant Museum of English Rural Life and later the Language Laboratory.

SECTION FIVE

Transport

THE FOUR HORSESHOES, Basingstoke Road, c. 1890. A loaded wagon waits, the horses patiently feeding, while the carter takes his refreshment inside. Used for heavy haulage of all kinds, this type of agricultural wagon was a masterpiece of the carpenter's and the wheelwright's art.

THE CARRIER'S CART. In 1900 there were no fewer than 94 carriers serving the villages around Reading. Thomas, the Burghfield carrier, who ran on alternate days from The Sun, Castle Street, not only carried goods and the occasional passenger, but would also undertake shopping for his customers.

BUTLER & SONS' beers, wines and spirits were delivered by horse-drawn van and by handcart. These delivery vehicles were photographed outside the Chatham Street premises around 1902.

HEELAS STEAM TRACTION ENGINE, 1912/13, used for furniture removals. Steam power proved ideal for hauling heavy loads over unmade roads. Here no fewer than three formerly horse-drawn pantechnicons are in tow.

H. & G. SIMONDS' STEAM LORRY, c. 1924. Whilst the cost of steam haulage was considerably less than that of horse power, steam vehicles were more cumbersome in use and had a shorter range than the motor lorry.

CAVERSHAM SUNDAY SCHOOL OUTING, 1911. A ride behind the traction engine provided an added thrill for the children.

THE ADULTS, HOWEVER, PREFERRED THE CHARABANC. A Fiat open tourer charabanc of 1922 operated by Royal Blue Motors, Horncastle Garage, Bath Road. At the wheel, the proprietor, Mr J. West.

SIMONDS' LOADING BAY, 1920. The stable-yard is almost entirely taken over by motor lorries.

THE LATEST ADDITION TO OUR TRANSPORT— DENNIS AND TRAILER.

AN ADDITION TO THE HUNTLEY, BOORNE & STEVENS FLEET. A Dennis lorry and trailer of the 1930s.

STEAM POWER AT H & P. Fireless locomotive No. 1 and driver, Mr Bill Pemberton. Charged with high pressure steam from a mains supply, two of these little engines worked in and around the factory without risk of fire or contamination. Built by Bagnall of Stafford in 1932, they worked until 1970. No. 1 has been preserved and is to be seen at the Great Western Railway Society's sheds at Didcot.

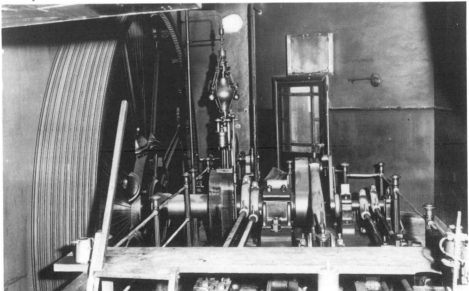

STATIONARY STEAM. 'Alice', one of three steam engines which powered the machinery of the factory. Built in 1882, this engine ceased work in 1927, but was recalled in 1947 when, coupled to an alternator, she supplied electricity to the factory at a time of severe fuel shortage and power cuts.

THE READING TRAMWAY COMPANY. Formed in 1878, this privately-owned company operated a service of horse-drawn trams between Brock Barracks and Palmer Park. The poor condition of the horses was a frequent cause for complaint.

THE FORMAL OPENING OF READING'S ELECTRIC TRAMWAYS, 22 July 1903, the Mayoress having switched on the current at the Mill Lane Depot and declared the tramway open. There followed a procession of trams, many decorated, the leading car being driven by the Mayor, Alderman A.H. Bull.

TROLLEYBUSES REPLACED THE TRAMS between 1937 and 1939. A line of the 'whispering giants' stand ready at the Mill Lane Depot early on a Monday morning before beginning their week's work.

READING'S LAST TROLLEYBUS *en route* for the depot for the last time, 3 November 1965. Vehicle No. 144, built in 1949 for the Whitley Wood route, is now preserved at the Westgate Trolleybus Museum near Doncaster.

STEAM PLEASURE LAUNCHES. In Victorian and Edwardian days, river trips were very much in demand by summer visitors to the Thames. A popular afternoon's excursion was from Caversham Lock to Sonning and back.

THE LARGER RIVER STEAMERS, several of which were operated by Reading's boat building and hire companies, were a perennial favourite for firms' outings and organised excursions. Built in 1908, Cawston's steamer *Majestic* could accommodate over 300 passengers.

FREIGHT TRAFFIC ON THE KENNET. Thames barges being loaded with casks and crates at Simonds' Brewery wharf. c. 1925

RIDLEY'S TIMBER YARD, c. 1900. A great deal of Reading's timber was transported by river from the London docks.

THE GREAT WESTERN RAILWAY played a major part in the growth of Reading and was as important to the town as the roads and waterways. A stopping train at Tilehurst Station, 1925, hauled by 'Saint' Class 4–6–0, No. 2986 *Robin Hood*.

NON-STOP THROUGH READING. 'The Cheltenham Flyer', the Great Western's record-breaking express in drab wartime livery, thunders through Reading Station, 1945.

Reading at War

THE ROYAL BERKS YEOMANRY CAVALRY in full (dismounted) dress, 1898. The uniform jacket was scarlet with blue facings, the trousers blue with a broad red stripe. The helmet plume and sword belts were white.

THE BERKSHIRE YEOMANRY (READING SQUADRON) in khaki field dress, 1910. Formed as an independent cavalry unit, the Yeomanry has since served as part of the Camel Corps, Machine Gun Corps and Royal Artillery.

PRIVATE FREDERICK WILLIAM POTTS of the 1/1st Berkshire Yeomanry (Territorial Force) was not only the first citizen of Reading to be awarded the Victoria Cross in the Great War, but was also the first yeomanry soldier to win the highest award for valour.

Severely wounded whilst taking part in an attack on the Gallipoli peninsula in August 1915, Private Potts, although able to return to safety, remained for over 48 hours in no man's land close to the Turkish trenches, caring for a soldier of his regiment who was so badly injured as to be unable to move. Fixing a shovel to the equipment of his wounded comrade and using this as a sledge, he dragged him over 600 yards under heavy enemy fire back to the British lines.

THE WAR HOSPITALS. In March 1915, the military took over the Borough Workhouse and Infirmary (Battle Hospital), together with a number of schools, for the treatment and care of some of the hundreds of wounded and sick men from the battlefields of Belgium and France.

MEDICAL AND SURGICAL STAFF of the Reading War hospitals. With some 1700 beds under his control, the commandant, Lt.Col. E.A. Hanley, built up a staff of doctors drawn mainly from the Royal Army Medical Corps and augmented by specialists from civilian hospitals.

UNLOADING THE WOUNDED AT READING STATION. Brought by hospital train from Dover, the wounded were conveyed by ambulance, or occasionally by private car, to the military hospitals in the area.

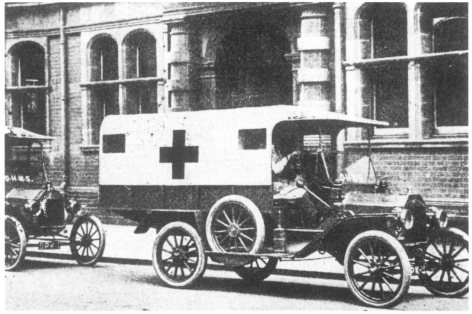

RED CROSS AMBULANCES. Reading's Wellington Club donated two motor ambulances for the use of the county regiment. It was agreed that these should be used locally, until such time as they could be used in a formation of which the Royal Berkshire Regiment formed a part.

PATIENTS AND STAFF, INNISCARRA AUXILIARY HOSPITAL, Bath Road. Established in 1915, this VAD hospital, under commandant Mrs Phyllis Henderson, accommodated up to 50 convalescent servicemen.

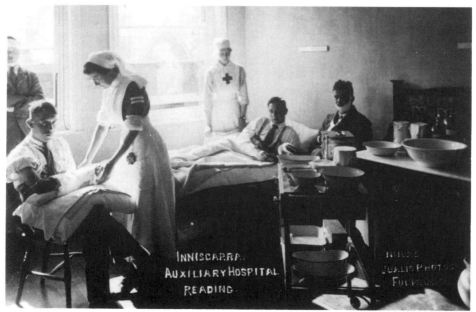

INNISCARRA. Soldiers undergoing treatment, 1916. The auxiliary hospitals were well supported by the people of Reading who did much to raise funds for comforts for the wounded.

HOSPITALITY AND ENTERTAINMENT of all kinds were provided by local people for those servicemen who were on the way to recovery. River trips with refreshments and sometimes a concert party on board were much enjoyed. The Thames steamer *Majestic* about to depart with a full complement of convalescent soldiers and voluntary helpers.

A PICNIC ON PEPPARD COMMON by motor cycle and side-car was the destination of this outing organised by Reading YMCA, July 1916.

RED CROSS NURSES preparing for a rally of Berkshire National Reservists and Red Cross detachments at King's Meadow on Saturday, 18 July 1914. Present were the Lord Lieutenant, J. Herbert Benyon Esq., and Mrs Benyon, Lady President of the county Red Cross. In less than three weeks the country would be at war with Germany.

RED CROSS RALLY at the Town Hall, 15 February 1919. Hostilities at an end, many of the detachments were in the process of disbanding. Crosses and certificates were presented to nurses for distinguished service and to those who had donated skin for grafting and blood for transfusion.

READING COMMUNAL KITCHEN, 1917. Set up by the Corporation at a time when food and fuel were in short supply, the communal kitchens offered daily a well-cooked meal for the poorer members of the community. The first of the communal kitchens at the former British Schools building in Southampton Street was supervised by Mr F.W. Marsh, meals superintendent to the Education Committee, seen in this photograph with his staff of eight.

UP-TO-DATE CATERING EQUIPMENT included a gas stove, roasting oven and steam boilers. A substantial hot 'take-away' meal was available at a cost of 6–8 pence per head.

WORLD WAR II brought the threat of enemy action to our homes. Members of Post D4, Caversham. Locally recruited, the ARP Service (later Civil Defence) was well-trained and organised to shoulder a wide variety of duties in the event of emergency.

THE HOME GUARD. Officers and men of the specialist wing of the Reading Battalion meet at Yeomanry House for the last time. It is 1944, the war is drawing to a close and their responsibility for the defence of the perimeter of Reading in case of invasion is at an end. Seated centre is the commandant, Lt. Col. G.S. Field TD; to his right Capt. H.H. Beck (adjutant); to his left, Capt. G. Astall.

SIMONDS BREWERY VOLUNTEER FIRE BRIGADE. Many of the larger companies formed their own fire-fighting units to protect their premises in case of fire through enemy action. Simonds built their own fire engine by mounting a pump and ladders on a works tractor.

THE WOMEN'S VOLUNTARY SERVICE formed in 1938 by Lady Reading to provide welfare assistance of all kinds in event of emergency. The staff of Reading's 'Food Flying Squad' on parade in St Mary's Butts in 1941. The vehicles were a gift from the people of Australia.

WORKERS PLAYTIME. To help maintain the morale of factory workers, the BBC broadcast lunchtime programmes of light entertainment from works canteens throughout the country. In January 1941, the venue was Huntley, Boorne & Stevens. Top of the bill was a youthful Bebe Daniels. In the supporting cast were Stainless Steven and Freddie Bamberger and Pam.

WAR SAVINGS. Everyone was encouraged to invest in National Savings to help the war effort. Huntley, Boorne & Stevens set their staff a target of £1500, the cost of an anti-tank gun. The score board shows nearly £300 saved to date.

AIR RAID DAMAGE, 10 February 1943. A single stick of bombs from a solitary enemy aircraft caused much damage in the town centre with serious loss of life. Rescue workers search the wreckage at the rear of Wellsteed's shop, Minster Street.

THE DEVASTATION IN FRIAR STREET. Messrs Blandy's office is destroyed by a direct hit; St Laurence's Church and the Town Hall are badly damaged.

THE VETERANS' ASSOCIATION on parade in St Mary's Butts, August 1912. Second and third from the right in the front row are Mr W. Brown (83) and Mr G. Watts, both of whom saw active service in the Crimea. The parade was inspected by General Sir Mowbray Thompson who distinguished himself in action at Cawnpore during the Indian Mutiny of 1857.

VETERANS OF A LATER WAR. The years having thinned their ranks, members of the Reading Branch of the Old Contemptibles and their wives joined with former comrades on Sunday 23 May 1969 for their last annual parade and march past at St Pauls.

People and Events – A Miscellany

THE STATUE OF KING EDWARD VII, which has stood since 1902 in Station Square, was presented to the town by Martin John Sutton as a permanent memorial of the new king's accession. Standing beside the nine feet high bronze statue in his studio at Fulham is the sculptor, Mr George Wade.

THE CORONATION OF KING EDWARD VII. 1902. The coronation, delayed for some months on account of the king's serious illness, was acclaimed with great public rejoicing and celebrations were organised on an elaborate scale. A grand procession through the town was held on 9 August, followed by entertainments, sports and fireworks.

TO COMMEMORATE THE CORONATION OF KING GEORGE V AND QUEEN MARY, June 1911, a commemorative tree is planted in the Forbury Gardens.

HRH THE PRINCE OF WALES, later to become King Edward VIII, visited Reading in June 1926. He opened the new Caversham Bridge and, in a crowded itinerary, visited a number of factories including Huntley, Boorne & Stevens where, accompanied by the managing director, Mr L. Victor Smith, he met members of the staff.

HIS TOUR OF THE FACTORY COMPLETED, the Prince leaves to visit the Royal Berks Hospital and the University.

AN INFORMAL STUDY of Rufus Isaacs KC, MP and his first wife, Alice. From humble beginnings and a varied early career, Rufus Isaacs, a man of great physical and mental vigour, established himself as a successful lawyer. His political leanings were towards the Liberals and he was returned as Member of Parliament for Reading in 1904, retaining the seat until his appointment as Lord Chief Justice in 1913. Upon his elevation to the peerage, he took the title 'Baron Reading'. In 1921 he was appointed Viceroy of India.

Whilst MP for Reading, Rufus Isaacs lived at Foxhill, Whiteknights, involved himself in many aspects of the life of the town and was generally well liked. He is reputed to have been a great supporter of Reading Football Club.

LLOYD GEORGE in 1910 delivers a fighting speech in support of Rufus Isaacs' candidature in the forthcoming by-election. The burning issue of the day was the proposed curtailment of the privileges of the House of Lords.

LORD READING in the robes of Lord Chief Justice of England. A portrait by local photographer, Walton Adams.

THE MASONIC LODGES of the county were not least among the benefactors of the Royal Berks Hospital. Crowds gather to witness the rare event of a public procession by the Masons.

THE RT. HON. LORD AMPTHILL, Pro Grand Master of England, presides over the ceremonial laying of the foundation stone of new buildings at the hospital, February 1911.

RAMBLING AND HIKING were popular social activities in the years between the wars. Carefree members of the West End Strollers, on a Sunday walk in July 1933, cluster around the Stratfield Saye-Silchester signpost.

MOTOR CYCLING was popular among young people in the 'Thirties. Here members of the South Reading Motor Cycle Club relax after a Sunday afternoon ride, 1932.

THE READING TEMPERANCE CHORAL SOCIETY. Under the leadership of their conductor, Mr W.F. Drew, the society achieved success after success. In 1939, the choir gained first place at the National Temperance Choral Union at Alexandra Palace.

READING ARCHERS. Formed in 1949 by a group of enthusiasts, the first matches took place under rather primitive conditions. Although in their first season a pile of straw bales served as a butt, the state of the 'gold' of the target is indicative of some pretty accurate shooting.

READING ARCHERS' FIRST OPEN SHOOT, 1952. Within a couple of years, the club was sufficiently strong to organise a shoot open to all comers at the Greyhound Stadium, Oxford Road.

READING REGATTA, 1927. The Reading University First Eight. Cole (bow), Clarke, Compton, Webb, Gildemeister, Rowe, Fidler and Trehane (stroke). The broad sweep of the Thames provides ideal conditions for competitive rowing.

WINTER BATHERS, Christmas 1908. These hardy beings seem happier in the water than out, whatever the weather.

TARGET SHOOTING with the small-bore air rifle was very popular in the years before World War I, with competitions organised on a league basis. The champions at the end of the 1909–10 season were the team from the Crown, Caversham.

THE SHOOTING TITLE was taken the following year by the team from the Plasterers' Arms, Newtown.

THE BAND OF THE READING CORPS OF THE SALVATION ARMY, 1882. The corps was formed in March 1881, its meeting place a former boat-house by the Kennet at Fobney. Later that year the corps moved to a specially-built temple in William Street, and in 1906 to the Citadel in St Mary's Butts.

THE READING CITADEL BAND, 1921. Four members of the band of 1882 appear in this photograph. Two, Charles Beale (front row, fourth from right) and Jack Smith (front row, end right), are still active musicians.

BOY SCOUTS OF THE READING (JUNIOR YMCA) TROOP, 1920, at their HQ, Garrard Hall. The movement, which was very popular among boys of all ages, was well supported in Reading.

THE WOLF CUBS of the YMCA Pack are presented with their ceremonial totem pole, 1921.

GUIDES AND BROWNIES. The 3rd Reading Company celebrates its 21st birthday, 1939.

PARADE OF THE STANDARDS. Berkshire Girl Guides parade before the Chief Guide, Lady Baden Powell, at the County Rally held at Sol Joel's Recreation Ground, 1945.

THE VOLUNTEERS. Reading's volunteer fire brigade on parade in the abbey ruins c. 1890. Formed in 1871, the Volunteers gave sterling service in and around Reading until 1893 when fire-fighting became the sole responsibility of the Corporation. On several occasions this steam fire engine was transported by rail to give assistance at fires in other towns.

CAVERSHAM FIRE BRIGADE. Resplendent in full dress uniform and brass helmets, the brigade mans the horse-drawn escape. The Caversham Brigade had its headquarters in Gosbrook Road with sub-stations at Caversham Heights and Emmer Green.

THE READING CORPORATION FIRE BRIGADE. The Corporation purchased its first two motorised fire engines in May 1912. The engine was built by Dennis, the wheeled escape by Bailey Ltd.

FIRE AT TYLE MILL. The mill, one of the largest in Berkshire, was totally destroyed by a fire probably caused by inflammable dust, on the night of Saturday 18 July 1914. The fire brigade was summoned by phone and was on the scene within half an hour. The fire engine from Englefield also attended.

THE THAMES IN FLOOD, 1947. A rapid thaw after a prolonged period of frost and snow caused the worst flooding for fifty years. The scene at the junction of Gosbrook Road and Washington Road where deliveries of milk and food had to be made by boat.

PALM SUNDAY, 1909. The clergy and congregation went in procession with the Blessed Sacrament for the first time in Reading since the Reformation. Following strong protest from certain sections of the Protestant faith, the Watch Committee banned future processions, but, after lengthy argument and a reference to the Home Secretary, the prohibition was rescinded.

THE GENERAL STRIKE, 1926. The Trades Union Movement was strong in Reading and demonstrations of workers' solidarity well supported. The local strike headquarters being at the Trades Union Club in Minster Street, the Market Place offered a convenient venue for larger meetings. Here the strikers are addressed by Ben Russell JP, branch secretary of the National Union of Gasworkers and General Workers (today the General and Municipal Workers Union).

A CONSTABLE OF THE READING BOROUGH POLICE, 1921. From 1836 until amalgamation in 1968 to form part of the Thames Valley Police, the maintenance of law and order within the Borough was the responsibility of Reading's own police force. The officer in this photograph is on point duty at Whitley Pump.

CAPT. J.S. HENDERSON, CHIEF CONSTABLE, with senior officers of the Borough police force, 1910. Retiring in 1923 after 26 years in the post, he was Reading's longest serving Chief Constable.

READING'S FIRST WOMEN POLICE OFFICERS, appointed in 1916, were replaced in 1919 by Miss Campbell and Miss King (seen above) who served until their retirement in 1940. In addition to her normal duties, Miss King (right) also served as part-time probation officer.

THE BOROUGH POLICE STATION AND COURTS, Valpy Street. Formerly part of the University College, the premises were acquired by the Corporation when the college moved to London Road. The new police station replaced the old building beside the Kennet at High Bridge.

THE COURT ROOM, 1912. The lecture hall readily lent itself to conversion to a courtroom. Both the magistrates court and the Borough quarter sessions sat here, the former until its transfer to purpose-built premises in the newly completed civic centre.

MOTOR-CYCLE PATROL. Recognising the need for mobility, the force took delivery in 1928 of two BSA motor cycle combinations for patrol work. These, together with the Chief Constable's Humber Snipe motor car, comprised the Motorised Division.

READING GAOL BY READING TOWN immortalised by Oscar Wilde in 'The Ballad of Reading Gaol'. Built in 1844 on the site of the former house of correction, Reading Gaol flourishes still. The original gatehouse, seen here shortly before demolition in 1973, is said to have been modelled on the entrance to Warwick Castle. Reading's last public execution took place on the flat roof in 1862.

THE PRISON viewed from the roof of Huntley & Palmer's, 1926. The prison was at this time empty, but held in reserve lest the need arise. The tower on the main building is for ventilation purposes. The turrets at the four corners of the wall served both as staff quarters and as defensive positions.

'E' WING. Until 1915, this detached block housed female prisoners. The matron, who lived in the corner turret, could gain access to her quarters only through the main cell block. This wing and the adjoining laundry buildings were demolished in 1970.

The Countryside Around

OXFORD ROAD, TILEHURST. Prior to widening in 1917, Oxford Road was but a tree-lined country lane leading to Pangbourne.

KENTWOOD HILL looking northwards across the Thames Valley, c. 1908. A truly rural scene at a time when country walks were within easy reach of the town centre.

PURLEY. 'The Short'. Part of the shanty town which grew up beside the village in the '30s in consequence of a property company offering small freehold plots at a bargain price of £5.

PANGBOURNE. In the background, the church of St James the Less. In the foreground, Church Cottage, the home of Kenneth Grahame, author of *The Wind in the Willows*. To the left are the flint walls and conical roof of the former village lock-up.

THE BRIDGE OVER THE PANG. In 1895 the river, which was renowned for its trout, appeared much wider than is the case today.

PANGBOURNE REACH at the turn of the century. A peaceful stretch of water and a quiet lane where, despite the intrusion of a row of late-nineteenth-century houses known locally as 'The Seven Deadly Sins', heron and kingfisher, moorhen and vole were still to be seen.

ST PETERS CHURCH, CAVERSHAM, c. 1900, from the river. To the right, with gardens running down to the water, is the Old Rectory.

THE GRIFFIN INN, CAVERSHAM, before rebuilding in 1900. Thames eels from the eel bucks to the rear of the premises were popular with local customers.

THE MAIN ENTRANCE TO CAVERSHAM COURT. Formerly the home of the Lay Rectors of Caversham and known as the Old Rectory. In 1916, when the right of the occupant to tithes lapsed, the house became known as Caversham Court. The property was demolished in 1933 and today only the old stable block and the riverside gazebo remain.

THE LIBRARY, CAVERSHAM. Established in 1907, the Free Library offered a lending service and reading room for the residents of Caversham which, prior to 1911, was independent of Reading.

THE WARREN, CAVERSHAM. This riverside road was built by Sir Richard Blount in around 1600 to afford better access to Mapledurham House. The name derives from the estate rabbit warren nearby which helped provide meat for the table.

8868 SONNING VILLAGE.

SONNING in the years before the Great War was an active, self-sufficient village, described by Jerome K. Jerome as having 'every house smothered in roses'.

Sonning Bridge and White Hart, near Reading

SONNING BRIDGE. The brick bridge with its eleven arches dates from the eighteenth century, but there has been a river crossing here from earliest times. The White Hart Hotel with its landing stage is reputed to stand on the site of the former ferryman's house.

ST PETER'S CHURCH, EARLEY, in 1902. Prior to the consecration of this church in 1844, the people of Earley had to travel to Sonning to attend services.

WOKINGHAM. The Town Hall and Market Place c. 1900. Once famous for its sales of poultry, the market had by this time diminished in importance.

CALCOT HOUSE built in 1795 by John Blagrave on the site of an earlier mansion. The estate was sold in 1929 and the park, once regarded as the most beautiful in the county, was laid out as a golf course, the mansion being used as the club house.

A CONTRAST IN ARCHITECTURAL STYLE. Wyfold Court, now part of Borocourt Hospital, was built in the 1870s for the cotton magnate, Edward Hermon. Of red brick with ornamentation in yellow and blue, the building is described by Nicolaus Pevsner as 'Nightmare Abbey in spirit'.

9016. The Pond. Three Mile Cross. near Reading.

THREE MILE CROSS, made famous by Mary Mitford who lived here for many years, was even at the turn of the century separated from Reading by open country. The duck pond by the green at the corner of Church Lane has long since disappeared.

THE KENNELS OF THE SOUTH BERKS HUNT, Long Lane, Purley, whence they moved in 1910 from World's End near the junction of the Bath and Burghfield Roads. Due to the growth of urban Reading, the kennels were transferred in 1955 to Mortimer.

MORTIMER STATION, 1863. The crowd on the platform has assembled to welcome Prince Edward (later King Edward VII) and Princess Alexandra. Opened in 1848, the line from Reading to Basingstoke was laid in broad gauge. Later a third rail, which is visible in this picture, was laid to enable standard gauge trains to run.

ROAD BUILDING, 1910. To provide work for some of the unemployed men of the district, the road from Mortimer to Burghfield Common was diverted around Warennes Wood.

GRANNY BALL, an unmarried lady who lived during the latter years of the last century in a thatched cottage near Mortimer Brewery. She brought up three orphan children, two girls and a boy. She was kind to the children and is remembered with affection. The photo shows her with one of the girls. A canary in its cage hangs on the outside wall.

ACKNOWLEDGEMENTS

This collection of photographs could never have been put together without the kind co-operation of the following people who have made available to me a great deal of valuable material from their private collections, or who have helped and advised me in a hundred different ways:

Dr A.M. Barr, Royal Berks Hospital • Berkshire Girl Guides Association Archives
The Berkshire Yeomanry Museum, Windsor • The British Red Cross Society
The British Trolleybus Society • Broadbear Bros. Ltd • Dr. T.A.B. Corley
Mr W.F. Champion • Courage Central Ltd • Mr Nigel Crompton • Mr A. Drew,
Weldale Motors Ltd • The Fire Brigade Society • J.A. Gafford Esq JP
Mr Roger Garrick • Huntley, Boorne & Stevens Ltd • Mr K. Jerome
Mr Denis Jones • The John Lewis Partnership • Mrs E. McMullin • Mr J.K. Major
Marks & Spencer plc • Milwards Shoes Ltd • Andrew and Helen Moglestue
The Mortimer Local History Group • The Headmaster, New Town School
The Headmistress, Queen Anne's School, Caversham • The late Mr F. Padley
Miss Sue Read • Reading Archers • Reading Museum and Art Gallery
The Headmaster, Reading Blue Coat School • The Headmaster, Reading School
The Headmistress, St Joseph's Convent School • The Science Museum Library,
South Kensington • Reading YMCA • The Salvation Army (Reading Central
Corps) • Mrs V. Sherbourne • Sirrel's Second Hand, Oxford Road
Suttons Seeds Ltd • Mr A. Taylor C.Eng., M.Inst.E. • Mr J. Taylor ARPS
The Thames Valley Police • Mr B. Turner, Church Crookham • The University of
Reading • Mr R. Walker • Mr Ray West • Woolworth Ltd. • The Women's Royal
Voluntary Service

Finally, but by no means least, I must acknowledge the encouragement, support and infinite patience afforded me by my wife, Mary, throughout the months spent preparing this book.